THE URBANA FREE LIBRARY

W9-AEL-070

DISCARDED BY THE
URBANA FREE LIBRARY

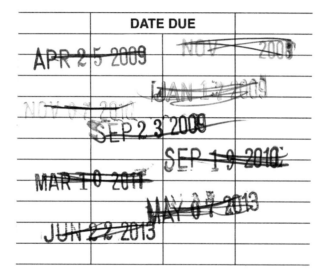

DATE DUE

APR 2 5 2009	NOV 2008
NOV 2010	JAN 1 2009
SEP 2 3 2009	
	SEP 1 9 2010
MAR 1 0 2011	
	MAY 0 7 2013
JUN 2 2 2013	

THE URBANA FREE LIBRARY

TO RENEW MATERIALS CALL
(217) 367-4057

Cooperation

Kimberley Jane Pryor

Marshall Cavendish
Benchmark
New York

URBANA FREE LIBRARY

This edition first published in 2009 in the United States of America by Marshall Cavendish Benchmark.

Marshall Cavendish Benchmark
99 White Plains Road
Tarrytown, NY 10591
www.marshallcavendish.us

All rights reserved. No part of this book may be reproduced or utilized in any form or by any means electronic or mechanical including photocopying, recording, or by any information storage and retrieval system, without permission from the copyright holders.

All Internet sites were available and accurate when sent to press.

First published in 2008 by
MACMILLAN EDUCATION AUSTRALIA PTY LTD
15–19 Claremont St, South Yarra 3141

Visit our Web site at www.macmillan.com.au or go directly to www.macmillanlibrary.com.au

Associated companies and representatives throughout the world.

Copyright © Kimberley Jane Pryor 2008

Library of Congress Cataloging-in-Publication Data

Pryor, Kimberley Jane.
    Cooperation / by Kimberley Jane Pryor.
       p. cm. — (Values)
    Includes index.
    ISBN 978-0-7614-3124-4
    1. Cooperativeness in children—Juvenile literature. 2. Helping behavior in children—Juvenile literature. I. Title.
    BF723.C69P79 2008
179'.9—dc22

                                                    2008001617

Edited by Helena Newton
Text and cover design by Christine Deering
Page layout by Raul Diche and Domenic Lauricella
Photo research by Naomi Parker and Legend Images

Printed in the United States

Acknowledgments
The author and the publisher are grateful to the following for permission to reproduce copyright material:

Front cover photograph of friends building a sandcastle courtesy of Photos.com

Photos courtesy of:
Corbis RF, **25**; Digital Vision/Getty Images, **17**, **26**; Photodisc/Getty Images, **15**; iStockphoto.com, **3**, **11**; © Ana Abejon/iStockphoto.com, **24**; © arpiaphoto.com/iStockphoto.com, **5**; © Ronald Bloom/iStockphoto.com, **20**; © geotrac/iStockphoto.com, **29**; © bonnie jacobs/iStockphoto.com, **8**, **12**; © Tomaz Levstek/iStockphoto.com, **30**; © Sean Locke/iStockphoto.com, **14**, **16**; © marmion/iStockphoto.com, **9**; © Carmen Martinez Banús/iStockphoto.com, **10**; © Christopher Pattberg/iStockphoto.com, **28**; © Josef Philipp/iStockphoto.com, **19**; © Julián Rovagnati/iStockphoto.com, **21**; © Marzanna Syncerz/iStockphoto.com, **4**; © 2008 Jupiterimages Corporation, photo by Radius Images, **18**; Photodisc, **13**, **23**; Photos.com, **1**, **6**; Stockbyte, **27**; Stockdisc, **7**; Thinkstock Royalty-Free, **22**.

While every care has been taken to trace and acknowledge copyright, the publisher tenders their apologies for any accidental infringement where copyright has proved untraceable. Where the attempt has been unsuccessful, the publisher welcomes information that would redress the situation.

For Nick, Ashley and Thomas

1 3 5 6 4 2

Contents

Glossary words

When a word is printed in **bold**, you can look up its meaning in the Glossary on page 31.

Values

Values are the things you believe in. They guide the way:

- you think
- you speak
- you **behave**

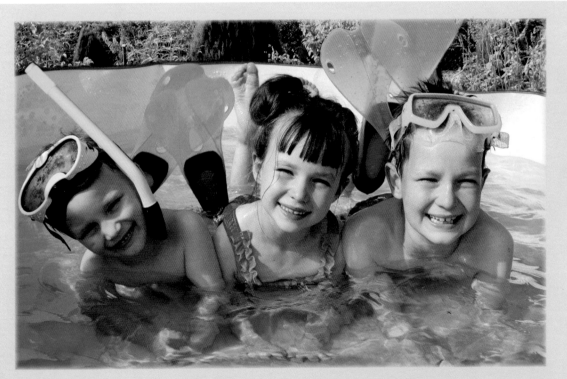

Values help you to play happily with friends in a pool.

Values help you to decide what is right and what is wrong. They also help you to live your life in a **meaningful** way.

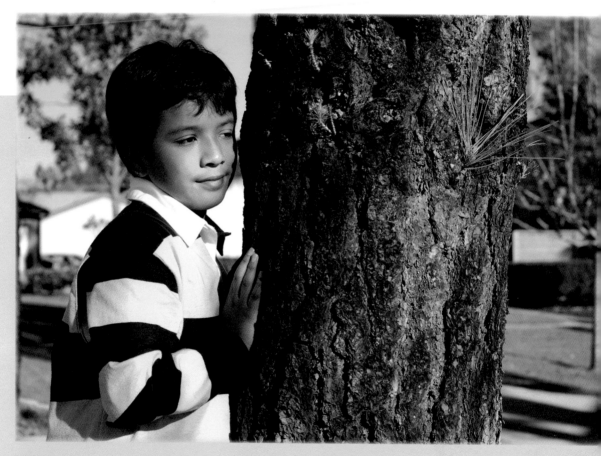

Values help you to follow the rules when playing hide and seek.

Cooperation

Cooperation is working together. It is teaming up with another person or other people to do or make something.

Friends often work together to build sandcastles.

Cooperation is also being helpful. It is giving **assistance** to people when they need it.

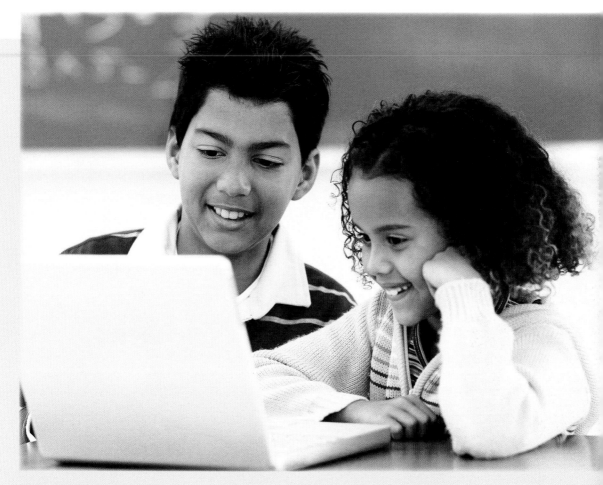

It is helpful to show someone how to use a new computer program.

Cooperative People

Cooperative people are **willing** to do what others ask them to do. They follow the **instructions** given for an activity or job.

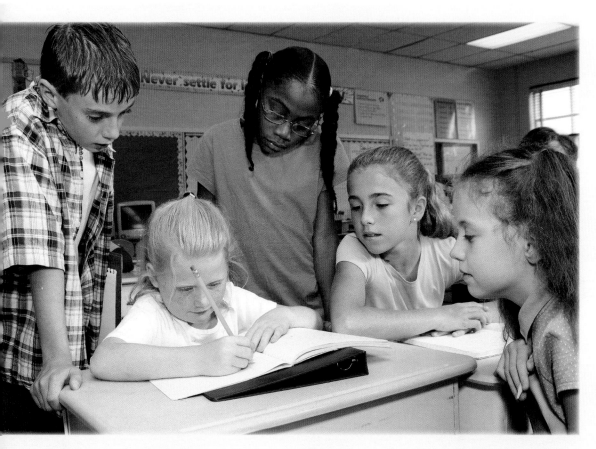

Cooperative students listen carefully and follow their teacher's instructions.

Cooperative people find ways to **solve problems**. They try to get on well with their family, friends, and neighbors.

Cooperative neighbors talk to one another about community problems.

Cooperating with Family

In a family, people cooperate by being kind to each other. They listen to each other and help each other out.

It is kind to help your younger sister learn to read and write.

Family members cooperate by sharing the jobs around the house. Some jobs are done more easily when two or more people work together.

This brother and sister work together to rake leaves.

Cooperating with Friends

Friends cooperate when they work together. When friends work on school projects together, they listen to each other's ideas. They also share the work.

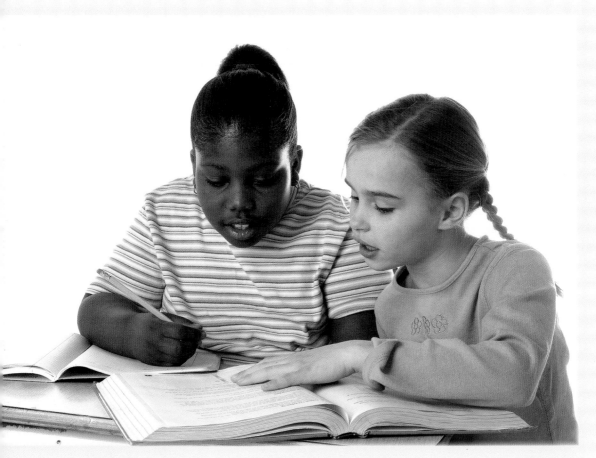

It is fun to work on a project with a friend.

Friends also cooperate when they play together. They share toys and take turns at the playground.

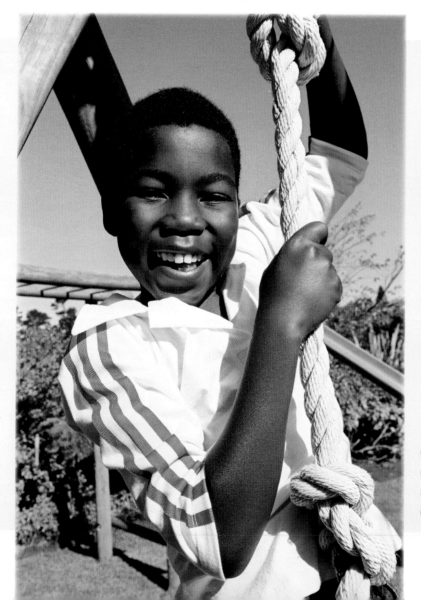

Letting everyone have a turn on the swing shows cooperation.

13

Cooperating with Neighbors

Cooperative people are **thoughtful** toward their neighbors. They do not make loud noises that might disturb their neighbors.

It is thoughtful to write to your neighbors if you are planning a large party.

Neighbors often cooperate by taking care of things in their neighborhood. Sometimes they work together to clean and fix their local school or community center.

Sometimes neighbors work together to plant a community garden.

Ways To Cooperate

There are many different ways to cooperate with your family, friends, and neighbors. Following instructions is a good way to start being cooperative.

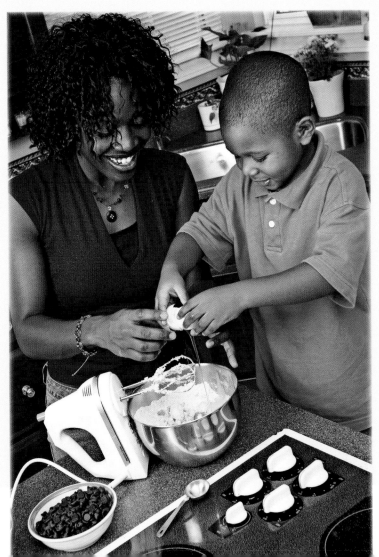

You can learn how to break an egg when you follow instructions.

Doing an activity with a partner is another way to practice cooperation. Being helpful is also part of being cooperative.

Partners need to cooperate when they run together in a three-legged race.

Following Instructions

Following instructions is one way to cooperate with others. You can learn new things when you follow the instructions of family members or teachers.

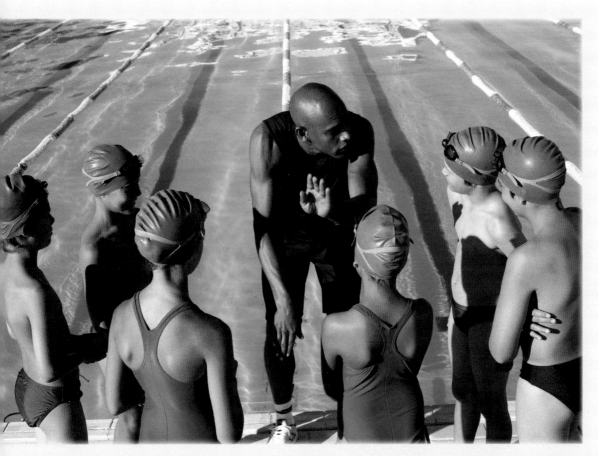

Following your swimming teacher's instructions helps you learn to swim.

Written instructions can tell you how to play a game or put a toy together. They can also tell you how to use the toy properly and safely.

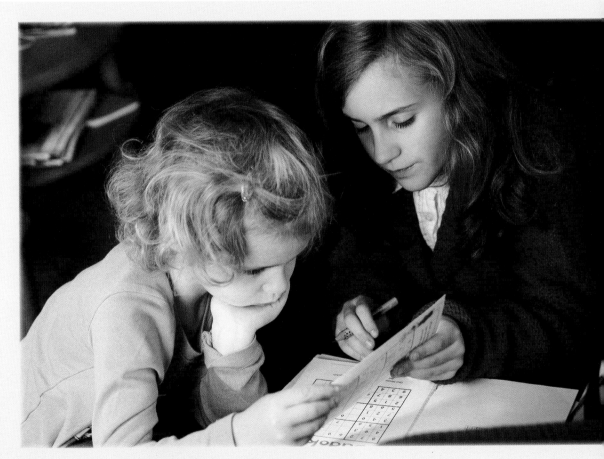

Following written instructions with someone else can help you to practice cooperation.

Sharing

Sharing is another way to cooperate with others. Some people are very good at sharing. They share their favorite toys with their friends.

It is kind to bring your favorite ball to the park to share with friends.

Brothers and sisters need to cooperate when they share a bedroom. They need to work together to keep the bedroom clean and tidy.

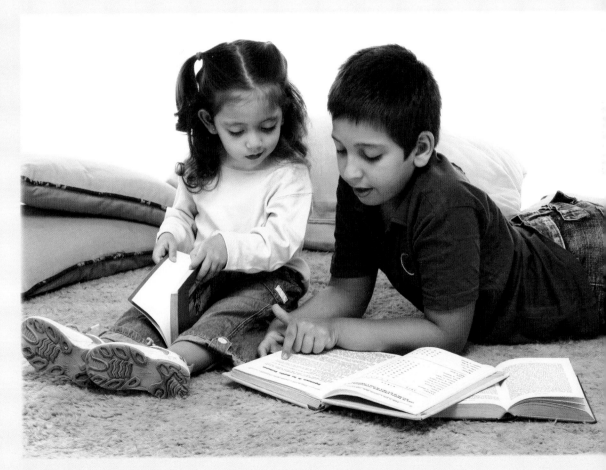

Brothers and sisters sometimes enjoy sharing books.

Working with Others

Many people find that they do better work when they work with others. A group of people can share their skills to create something new.

These people are enjoying working together.

When they work together, people can teach each other new **skills**. They can also learn new skills from each other.

Students share their skills when they paint a mural together.

Being on a Team

People often need to work as part of a team. On a sports team, players cooperate by following the rules of the game.

Soccer players cooperate by doing what their coach asks.

Players also cooperate by making sure that everyone gets a turn. When they take their turn, they do their best so that the team does well.

All the members of a basketball team need to work together.

Helping Others

Cooperative people like helping others. If they see a person in need, they offer to help.

Helping a family member search for a lost toy is a way to be cooperative.

Cooperative people help when someone asks them to help. They also ask for help when they need it.

You can help a classmate by turning the pages of a book while she reads.

Solving Problems

Solving problems is part of cooperation. Cooperative people think of different ways to solve a problem. Then they choose one way and try it.

Brainstorming is thinking of lots of different ways to solve a problem.

Cooperative people do not shout or hurt others when they feel angry. They calm down and think before they say or do anything. This helps them to solve problems.

Taking a deep breath or counting to ten helps people to calm down when they are angry.

Personal Set of Values

There are many different values. Everyone has a personal set of values. This set of values guides people in big and little ways in their daily lives.

Cooperation is an important value for construction workers to have.

Glossary

assistance   help

behave   act in a certain way

instructions   words that tell you how to do something or how to behave

meaningful   important or valuable

problems   things that are difficult to understand or fix

skills   abilities that help you to do activities or jobs well

solve   find the answer to

thoughtful   showing that you think and care about others

willing   ready and eager to help

Index